Solution Simulacra

Gloria Frym

OTHER BOOKS BY GLORIA FRYM

Homeless at Home
Distance No Object
How I Learned
By Ear
Back to Forth
Impossible Affection
Second Stories: Interviews with Women Artists

Solution Simulacra

Gloria Frym

UNITED ARTISTS BOOKS 2006

Some of these pieces appeared in slightly different versions in *Black Box; Big Bridge; Caprice; Exquisite Corpse; Gowanus Milk City; Gypsy Vergin; House Organ; Milk Magazine; Nth Position*, London, UK; *New American Writing; Nocturnes; The Muse Apprentice Guild; Times New Roman: Poets Oppose 21st Century Empire Anthology; Variant 2*, Vancouver, BC; *Skanky Possum; Women Studies Quarterly; Van Gogh's Ear*, Paris.

Profound gratitude again to the Fund for Poetry.

Cover image: "Waters of March" by Amy Trachtenberg; 2002, acrylic and enamel oil on canvas; 56″ x 26″. Courtesy of Brian Gross Fine Art, San Francisco

Book design:
   Cover, George Mattingly
   Interior, Noam Scheindlin

Author photograph: Dana Landau

First Edition
ISBN: 0-935992-39-1

United Artists Books
114 W. 16th Street., 5C
New York, N.Y. 10011

The war
you say
What war?

Let's call it
"The War of the Arabs"
so we can
refer to it later

Abdellatif Laâbi
from "In Praise of Defeat"
The World's Embrace

TABLE OF CONTENTS

For Julia, even more

OVERTURE

These poems were written in a country whose government invaded and bombed an already devastated Afghanistan, pre-emptively made war on Iraq, and declared the wars concluded only to continue bombing the "insurgents" during occupation. After September 11, 2001, the government of the United States commenced to terrorize its own citizens openly. The government also terrorized and tortured persons merely suspect of actions against the United States. Much of the rest of the world grew more bellicose and bent on suicidal martyrdom.

A perpetual war on terror preoccupied and distracted citizens from the myriad domestic maladies entrenching the United States, and provoked a fear far surpassing that of the cold war of the 1950s. Patriotism and old totalitarian tactics were freshly repackaged as new yet strangely familiar commodities. The government began to eviscerate a social contract it had once idealistically adopted from the Enlightenment.

Many of the writings in *Solution Simulacra* served as personal prophylaxis against the falsehoods of the daily news, which both magnified actions and minimized, even censored, active dissent against war and attempts to resolve conflict.

A rush of thoughts is the only conceivable prosperity that can come to us, Ralph Waldo Emerson offers, a sanctuary in this sad start to the 21st century.

OUT

Sudden power outage.
By candlelight the past looks better.
One didn't vote for George the lesser one simply
was thrown into the same room
history followed. During the holidays,
history comes to a head
more melancholy than sordid.
Before nixing the archives, move on
one is moving on, it's just the move on part
around the potholes. Christmas hands the past
back on a tarnished platter one wouldn't mind
shining up right about now instead of
receiving preposterous bulletins
from ports of authority. Don't your anti-
disestablishmentarian ears hear them?
Retorts felt strong as ox before.
Made oxtail soup every day. Please do me
the favor of not dousing the little light
allowed at this moment. One thinks one needs
something but one can live without it.
It's just a different life, filled with place cards
and sub-rosa rosettes and the shadows they cast.
War contracts for spring.
By summer, a whole civilization
is shattered and replaced by
not much. What's Milan showing next fall?
Morning is best, before mourning returns
one can handle power failure. Everyone sees
the blown apart, everyone eager to eat the pieces
right up, having no idea of how to resuscitate the heart.
The lights will come on again, one expects.
Every day is a year in the exaggerated dog.
One reserves one's bark for another thief
who enters by a crack in the window
stands over one's bed and watches one sleeping.

One awakes to the stranger. *And who the fuck might you be?*
The stranger flees in terror
at the sound of such a voice. Or:
One awakens to the desired. In the darkness
one is forbidden to look. If one abides by this myth
everyone lives happily ever in ahistorical bliss.

PLANS

The war had barely begun but colonialists plan ahead. Post-conflict structures were in place before the exact place was chosen. The heads on the shoulders of the colonialists are fatter than most. Just examine the dimensions of an 18-year-old private next to a 60-year-old rear admiral. Or his commander-in-chief. Use the measuring device approved by Goebbels to determine the size of the nose also.

Air-conditioned tanks rumble across the sand. My, what a comfortable war. There's a wet bar downstairs. Nothing one saw or heard, just a deck of cards and the dealer. In order to process your application, we must have the following: all documentation from everything you've ever done, plus everything you haven't done. Meanwhile, instead of a tank backing up and rolling over a life again, this year one promises to backhoe the grass, with all apologies to Whitman. Small garden beds, nothing king size, so the plants won't get too lonely without one another. One is anxious for victory and desires to provide a contribution to resolving the conflict between man and nature. Every night one will sneak out with a flashlight and pick the snails off the seedlings and throw them into on-coming traffic. One is sorry if this offends animal rights, but it makes vegetarians happy. This writing could be eaten instead of read if necessary. Here is arugula—if it goes wilty on you, just put it into a garlicky tomato sauce and throw that over pasta. Miner's lettuce is quite delicious too. Each artichoke costs about $5 if you count labor, and provides purple blossoms when it goes to seed. And it is of course priceless, uninsurable, unstable, non-pareil to the grower. That man in the hills with the vineyards, making his mash, is prohibited from selling it in his own restaurant. However, growing a radish, three eggplants, calendula is a still life while there is still life. One's pre-post-conflict structures are coming along nicely, don't you think? Yes, colonialize the backyard, march right in and take over. Tomatoes will have their own quarter, segregated from zucchini. In gardens, there is some good reason for apartheid. If you let the sweet peas reseed themselves, the next generation grows up pale pink. Plums will fall all over late summer, mooshing up everything, but that can't be helped. They are the princesses of the land and take up a lot of space and demand allegiance. Corrupt tribal leaders have claimed their stakes in Afghanistan and the place is no place, the people hobbling about on crutches, brick homes like Anazazi ruins. Remedy: start tourist industry. Visit the ruins empire has created. Feel proud. Even headless Buddhas, not for the faint of heart. I don't understand why I can't buy a burka in the surplus store. Did Milan or Paris get hold of them?

One is embarrassed about being on so many black lists. There are no black vegetables to grow except in a book whose author dreamed a house while never leaving it. But what can one do after a lifetime of sticking out one's tongue? Say ah, Gracie. Now I understand. I was supposed to keep it in my mouth or they'd cut it out.

Tearful spouses hug their enlistees one more time before the ship comes. All one sees is orphans as far as the future can go.

NEXT

Arousing deep suspicion   Not last verse or chapter   A terse masculine rhyme

    More war suns can't ameliorate   The sad liberation of no one   Victory's

Tasteless entrée   A fine blood soup and sand dusted oil cakes   Priapic

    Technophilia   The smashed cradle of the word   Starving after another

Lost   Foray   The emigrants took a vote   Which infant to throw off the boat

    Profits Recover Jobs Vanish Stocks Rise   "Looting is a way station

To liberty and freedom"   That was April this is Mother   May   I?

    Embedded press   Secret insomniac

A new emotion called Backwards   All words mean the reverse

    Hello inflicts a physical wound   Goodbye says we're coming to get you

MESSAGE INTERRUPTUS

Σ

Boo-hoo say the blues and so say I
ever. And so say the sky in spring if I
reads reflecting itself underneath
its surface. Does the sea see its green?
Only a we do. And take for color
an array of hues.
As you take a me for who one I is.
Unless blue interrupts your color schema.

A you left an I black and blue,
no slap slug ba boom
but [{(doubt]})????? tamper
with delicacy, an exquisite trans
human. Does some I strike
back? Words the weapons of mass d?
You betcha your blue collar with the lipstick
tell your tale, the stray ear stud
on the table. You got so many children
you don't know what to do.
Dis   arm   those arms
so wrapped around an unknown I.
Dislip those lips while you're at it.
Disremember all until surface beats out ripe.
Dis Dis Dis
And give the girl back the complete set of Billie H.
She needs it now, blue as black ever were

*   *   *

א

Rid the jewelry box of lapis lazuli, the darker color of all things too big to know. STOP.
The apocalypso right outside the door. STOP. Bring on the flamenco. STOP. For the rapture
is near. STOP A Christian invention, Jews cannot comply. STOP. There was no
rapture for them or the Africans. STOP.
Just movement. STOP.
Wandering into the heart of some STOP
place. Some person. Some. STOP.
Replace ~~beloved~~ with new unshared life, that cannot as objects hold
sentimentality. STOP. One could rip up the chemise or draw a woman on the pubic
area and scratch it out until DeKooning. STOP. Who would be I. STOP.
So what lips. STOP. A derangement alerts the birthday, still one is born. STOP.
How could it be that one loves a derangement. STOP.
It was the first breast one knew. STOP. And knows and knows and knows again. STOP
She came home one day and announced that her heart was on the wrong side. STOP.
All others one entered possessed the same malady. STOP.
A flower derangement. STOP. Please take me to Ikebana school. STOP.
Make a single leaf stand
for a whole season. STOP.
Born. Lived. Died. STOP.
Born. Live. STOP. Live. STOP.
Lived among the wars of spring. STOP.
The blossoms. STOP.
Younger now. STOP.
Awaiting the new. STOP.
No particular reply. STOP

* * *

Co war d   seducer   opening a wound   ed   country

The No Fly Zone(((((((((((((((((((((((((((((((())))))))))))))))))))))))))))))))

          doesn't that mean

Won't stop   until   silence   stops   all   not

          aware   of   fall
          out((((((((((((((((((((((((((((((

a you   in   you   hates

your   mirror [   ]
                                [   ]   here   put your face   here

what you   love   you   ab hor   you   need

          you   blur   faithlessly

all   you   touch   blues   to

          you

          you

          you

doesn't a you recall   how the Spanish undid

          and did

Queen Isabella   slept   on the bed

          of her   enemy   against the blue tiles   while Boabdil

stayed close   to   his mama   on that hill   in the Alpujarras

Lanjaron   Pampañeira   Bubion   Capileira   Orgiva

Salobreña   blue hydrangeas beyond profusion   where the plum

falls from the tree   and rolls   toward that you

sweetest

ever tasted   the goatherd   with his flock   on the highway

the bells   clanging into   the distant   Mediterranean
          at last

dipping into clear salt water   the white washed cities

against the blue

his sure navigation   why did he fail

that Moorish prince   that beautiful king   of

those who   loved   him   he refused to look   a
fleeing

sultan   an anti-Orpheus

surveying   Al-Andalus

as Mama   snarled   *weep like a woman*

for what you lost as a man

LOST EMPIRES

Dawn seemed as though it would never arrive. Yet the nights grew shorter after the solstice. The sky heavy and low, a mist like sweat in the air, a darkness sister to the proverbial. Distant prayers faintly heard from across oceans and centuries, a wail so slight yet so present. Would one's country march off to war only to become the laughing stock of the rest of the world? Self-destruction is the number one disease of empires. They have all had clogged arteries, cancer, brain tumors, bad lungs (from the smoking guns). They rise up having given birth to themselves and often suicide despite admonitions and attempts by their own citizens to save them. One's empire choking. One doesn't believe one's president who attends church, his slightly perfumed wife by his side, his daughters stoned out on downers. He read the Bible in Cliff's Notes. Forgot the part about gluttony as a sin. Fat-headedness isn't hormonal, it's caused by eating eating and eating. Fat cars eat oil, roads, other cars. One is tired of marching against something, one wants to march for something. If one makes no profits on one's non-existent stocks, can one receive some compensation in the form of monetary gain equivalent to what one would have had to pay in taxes if one had a portfolio? Dawn still doesn't dawn. In this hour, one must turn on all the house lights and read fictional accounts featured on the stage of the newspapers. Would they please print the long stories in serial installments every two weeks? The faint wailing of ancient prayers ceases. It is silent. And dawn has still not arrived. One is worried for the weather, the ice melting so fast where one has planned to exile the puppets and their puppetmasters. Perhaps one will have to devise another solution—shoot them into space and make them orbit the earth forever, watching from so many light years away what they did and what they could have done. If you have a better plan, please contact this page. Poetry accepts all subject matter. It is especially interested in the young. Their ideas are so fresh and agile. If one is recruited in one's youth, one might never march off to war. Though nothing is guaranteed, there are prophylactics. They sometimes burst, and one becomes pregnant with thought. Notice how many artists are fit and within their weight limit, and care little for war fat. Perhaps their gluttony for acknowledgement is a healthy aspect, perhaps their sins are transformed into objects that have no purpose but to exist. The record of this existence is the history of lost empires.

TRICK

The trick of happiness
       In a sad world
              Is no small trick

One who turns complications
       On their sides
              To see how they're

Made still seeks bliss
       In spite of known
              And documented side effects

Architects of doom
       Deception's weaponry
              Designed fear

Perverts love
       Nothing to be done with sadness
              Anger propels people vote

Happiness as superior
       For its fleeting yet acrobatic
              Potential

Cranes fly home in a V
       Do butterflies
              Terrorize their own

Dogs don't eat dogs' bones
       One tries to envision happy thoughts
              Snagged by little glitches in the outerwear

Yo sé que nunca besaré tus labios otra vez
       A trick to make the art appear

TROPIC BRIDE

When the poet says flowers he calls up
the missing flower in the bouquet
                              Baudelaire

The flower can't be worrying about food, can't be getting up and going over to the spigot and messing with the water hose. It isn't her job.

Hey you gardenia! The gardener can't be a flower while gardening, or how many heads do you have?

Troubled trope for incomparable times. And didn't one imagine a world in which one could be both tenor and vehicle? Change the rules to suit the ruling? Rather, the best one can count on is the infusion of comic dread. In a reign of terror, one has to live coming and going, down and up two tracks—more conscious—with better designed side view mirrors. *Objects are as close as they appear, perhaps closer*. Betting against the house, as they say, knowing the house always wins in the end. And here one is, in the middle, having to pretend endlessness.

Admittedly, time is always running out. Is there no remedy, no vaccination? But time is not a disease. Time is already a trope for death. Whole libraries have been constructed to house its antidotes, its amulets, its enemies.

KEEP YR DISTANCE

You've hired me to provide illustrious narrative. Seeing only what is arranged, it's hard to come up with a juicy story. The president says the public knows the difference between politics and reality. This statement has so disjuncted my tale that it must substitute reality for actuality. *If we'd thought we'd be here this long, we'd of never signed up*, no one said. *It's so hot our dog tags are branding our chests*, bemoaned no one else. *We're in the heart of the country, triple bypasses of the rules of war, and a triangle of fertile oil.*

Ok: Here's the scoop: We're dangling off the Euphrates where years ago men seined for carp. There are no tourists, hotels in neighboring cities rise for what people buy and sell. Persuaded by a confidence man, Melville shows up on the Tigris a century and a half late, double or nothing, any old trick to keep the game going. Tales swim through ponds and lakes, rivers and oceans to get out. True narrative escapes me; some grenade, some grenadine in the drinks and *they flee from me that sometime did me seke*. Characters float in and out of congressional paragraphs and arrive home in body bags.

Late at night, doors slam harder, foghorns moan microphonically by the harbor. The gulf, the one outlet to the sea, lonely as an only child. Knowing this, occupants might take precaution, but knowledge has little to do with time, so one goes ahead knowing and forgetting. Noise, like infection, spreads. War is a very loud sore that never scabs over due to wet cold hot muggy frozen thinly negotiable human conditions. Meanwhile we explore the idea. A feeling will do, but only what we know about feeling, as the page rejects direct contact and does not like to be held closely.

THIN CRUST

We were extremely hungry
We ate what was put in front of us
We drank what was offered
We were prisoners of oily folly
An upside down M is a W
The cradle of the universe may be Mars
Therefore we may all be Martians
Scientists said we were Africans
Poets only suspected radio transmission

We probed we explored the terrain
Of power bars death cultures which qualified us for further
Experiments in space spacing them out like
Missions then prisons new manifest destiny

Our Texan plans to send humans
To your place *Planet Armed Colony*
Country Patriot Insurgent Slave sorry for the foul language
Sorry if you're earless microbes
Nuclear reactors coming to a screen near you soon
Something living always extinguishes life
You gotta have a dream if you don't have a dream
Here on Earth bounty hunting
How do you like peanut butter
Foiled by lawless entities
Not responsible for the actions of its agents

Humans created conflicting heavens
Harps beards togas tests pearly gates
Throbbing revirginated souls
Pools of reflections lounging around reading
The stars

If you can't find a book what good is it?
Cavities braces busted ignition coils

Breyer horses action figures fraying
Towels trowels rusted
Drainpipes blocked with mud
House slipping off its rocker
One sock never finding its match
Easter basket Barbie limbs
Eggs ossified greenly by now
Radio Flyer wagon plastic laundry caskets
Bending mended duct tape
Bulbs that don't rise up and cry Bloom
Molly *Yes Yes Yes Yes*
I am Yours in my Andalusian dress
O that awful deepdown torrent and the sea the sea
Outgrown supposes cracked hoses
Washer dryer buyer sigher desire
Leaded dishes deferred wishes
Hold it buster! That was "a dream" Langston Hughes wrote
Battery operated neck vibrator

Homer homed homing homage home loan homeless
No Elliot Ness to round up
The usual suspects so much less fun
Than when we first had fun
Martians might be good
Naming rocks on sky rocketing properties
Your invisibility your incompatibility
With anything known as US
Here on Earth people have stopped looking
Eyes gouged out by excessive Googling
A tiny flashlight attached to our key rings
Helps us find the right latch
Unemployment rates interest
Flaccid like a you-might-know-what
If you are sleepy kleptons
Red dust in your fragile breezes
Would damage the delicate machinery

We really do have to clean up the library
These books won't give us any clue
To the future their spines brittle
Their thoughts cracked
Certain heads want to rid texts altogether
Just read the topical trends in percentages
Not even blab of the pave
So long and so déclassé
Too filled with content
During a winter of discontent
Right before the torrents of spring
Right after orange alert turns yellow then green

Are you given to song?
One celestial note could prove us wrong

IN PERPETUITY

The early bird with tinsel in her beak. This is how time passes and parents make their little nests. No longer a user of certain hygienic products, one now must supply one's child. The blood of love to come. Spring hovers close by. Nights shorten, buds dream. There seemed to be a break in the violence and now it will begin again. All is calm, all is bright just before the advance. Will any of the boys pick up a gun or will blast come from overhead, pilotless bombers bearing no bullets. One can now expect to be a veteran of many wars in one lifetime. No more yours and mine. Those who witness, those who drop in the markets, those who fly apart like blazing flower petals, those whose legs are blown off dancing, those who read in between the lines, on the front lines, hiding behind the fictional, stuffed with the emperor's stuffing, slicked with the sheik's grease, all concocted by the CEOs and their Pinocchios. They know ruin never ends.

MORPHOLOGY

Best friends morph to worst enemies. If you draw a line through a name, it will still be there and go away. So stop feeding the dog and he may sink his jaws into the government that starves him. The end could be detonated grudges. Work very hard to hear and not pay attention. *Attendez-vous*! We're leaving out the *s'il vous plâit* just now because your manners are despicable. Just as the news leaves out the news. Speaking of which, the enemies both profited greatly over stolen goods. There was always a fall guy. One could never hang up on him, he hung himself during a long rope. I want to be lassoed, and then released to graze the syllables. Of sound I speak, of speech I cannot say. I is going to continue to deblind the screen with violent strokes, even if the first writings are the first collateral damages. Reflections seem to lie behind the surface. The worst candidate for change is the one who knows too much. The one whose intelligence prevents him from alterations fits his once ill-fitting pants too well. Reveling in luxurious optimism when the castle's aflame. A Rome is burning now somewhere or about to. Do you have your fireproof smoke screens ready? Enough provisions to live about twelve minutes more than the next door neighbors? Then you can eat while you peek out the blinds and watch the little girls in white anklets pass by. How we vowed to cherish them. And now look what we've done.

BORN AND UNBORN

As one ally increasingly quotes from his sacred text, the other digs into medieval versions of his, and the two re-divide the world into yes and no. Whole centuries abolished, whole babies thrown out with the blood waters, whole women covered from head to toe in mourning clothes. Pledges of allegiance with codas concerning the born and unborn. As though the unborn would even want to be born the middle of this kiss me deadly. I heard one the other day gossiping to her twin, saying fuck that, you wanna live, go ahead, I'm going back home. Whatever one wakes up for in the morning one has to construct with precise architectural plans, then rip them up and redraw them, adding new doorways and windows. And spaces without name, so the four winged creatures can fly in and out in and out. Any contact with news blown in from behind the curtain is punishable by several days of dysphoria, low level, yet extant. It is the same for relatives of the lost. One believes one has accumulated the strength to face the fallout, yet just wait until the dust settles, the wind picks up and blows into those very open windows. One may know much less about the interior of the ally after many years than one knows about a stranger made familiar by a few hours, and yet, there is no screen with the stranger on which to project the great cinema. One could stand on one's head with conviction and recite the obstructions the other created to achieve his own justice. One dare not ask, how did such a paid ally become an enemy after so many profitable years.

MOCK SONG

Another day before   The NextWar   Rain likely

   Mockingbird tunes up

                Potable water   Not luck

Help   Some

                Picnic   These memorial horizons

                              Promised translucent
Now old thought

                In young clothes

Closed to them

                      All those in heaven

    Shake their heads

              Especially the collaterally

                           Damaged   Headless Buddhas

Shake whatever they can

                The Pope shakes his finger he's

                   God's lawyer and his client is

Dead   This war's got a II   After it   A child of 13

Will see it twice

Last time

During potty training   Oh young recruits

Always be wary of a man

Named for his father   Naming maims

Shoes to fill   Fill 'er up quick

Let us send our potatoes

Out to be mashed

Before duct tape shuts

Our million dollar bash   And we can't

Eat   The fresh and meaty   Result   Of every war

And don't forget

To seal the door

FACE VALUE

All night the wind blows horizontal rain, whipping the façade. If one were walking against this torrent, one would have to bend to it, to protect one's face. Palm trees, bamboo know what to do. Humans stay in their beds, prone to excitement. In an earthquake, a woman hid under her pillow. The tremor settled down, safety returned, why should she face it.   Each airport van incites surprise. One would open the door and the deceased, now undead, would stand with suitcase in hand, all face. Weapons of doubt destroyed and now peace reigns. Instead, a man with spit in his beard, drives up in a rusty corvette for a chat. Not the face that launched a thousand rowboats down a merrily merrily merrily. Rain begins again precipitously, falling in a vertical fashion. Why do people get the face they deserve? Why not another face that someone else deserves? One's face could be mistakenly placed on a body that didn't belong with it.   After a facial, the surface is red, inflamed from the fussing. Put the paper face up or down, one can never remember, these machines, each requiring a different position.   Still again, now sun.   In profile beautiful, one side belying the other, two-faced. Nothing in that face reveals anything other than itself.   Perhaps the eyes reveal the soul perhaps not, perhaps the soul is under construction. Countries engage in face-offs. One goes about one's business without a face. A face is for others to view.

WITH OR NOT

Either the world is of our making or we wait for it to unfold. Either we plan or someone has planned for us. Either there is indifference, which is punishment, or there is reception of our efforts. There could be a mixed reception, which would make us unhappy. Either we act or we observe actions. As long as we do not stand back and imagine all this is happening as we are watching, we retain our sanity. Once we disengage, we are lost. We breathe fully and our lungs function and we are unaware of the air. In this way we are found. Either it works or it doesn't. Or we pay for it to work. Either we concentrate or we disperse, it goes well or it doesn't. If it doesn't we are not. We want to be, therefore we will unite. This is the world of absolute wisdom, the world of the yes or the no. You see, there are a million ways of saying no and only one way of saying yes. At least for now. And now is all we have now. Later, it may change. We may not want what we want now. But at any given moment yes or no is imperative. Or it is not. Either you live or you die. If you blend the two, you are already dead. Either you are Yvonne or Ivan. If you are not Yvonne, you are someone else. You have a driver's license or you don't, you drive or you don't. You cannot drive a little, you cannot live a little, you cannot hold back on being born. Yes, millions try, the lunging forward and the receding. During the receding, rest approaches, but it is a restless rest, it is a sleepless sleep, a forward knife is easily replaced by a slow slide backwards into confusion, where you stay for some time until you have paid. Then you emerge, and the moment you begin, you're on you're way home. It may not seem so, but it is so. Check your records. Check the graphic accounts where the mathematics of your ascent is clearly evident by your attendance. If a chair loses an essential leg, it cannot seat. If a thought becomes an algebra, the unknown is not known. Let us quit this mucking about in the soggy zones. Either you do or you don't, either you will or you won't. One measure of doubt requires the subjunctive, the conditional, the indeterminate, which is not the simple present. In the present, things are. For example, "I just bought a new magazine," declares its existence. This is how you must function. In the simple declarative. Anything else confounds. Either you follow these instructions or you are lost. Either you believe or you don't. In some situations, you might, when it comes to the moment of truth, that's why it's the moment of truth. Imagine yourself when coverlets weigh heavy below your faint breath. Will you think of one nation under god or not?

DAWNLESS

In the slow horiscopical world would this dawnlessness involve a crying sky? A budding spring that folded back into itself, discontent, savvy, unwilling to flower merely to die into leaves. One war after another and so few intervals on the scale, as time sped up in order for death to occur rather than life. Twilight brings on the wine, the desire for peaceful repast. And then night tosses and turns, anticipatory for the very light that rejects the day. There were hours, what was done with them? Billions spent, lack of evidence, personnel deployed and destroyed. There was the film one took in, uplifting like a good brassiere. Nothing store bought would fit when dawn failed to arrive. Such a lapse brings on emotional incontinence in one, arctic rage in another. *God made our heads round so our thinking can change direction.* This shows some sense in nature, one thinks, nature evolves intelligently, as some humans may not. One recalls persons stupid to themselves, with no full-length mirror to confirm this condition. Content with what's on their plates, even if the cutlery is plated. Dawn still stalled. By this time, it was night by the clock, our glow-in-the-dark Lady of Guadalupe wept at the shocking lack of miracles. Homicides rose in direct proportion to layoffs. Suicides stood in the front lines ready to go out in a bang. Infanticides filled empty column space. Why should dawn want to face the day, considering its quiet, fragile light? Dawn can't save one civilization from unraveling, or another from erasing words for a living.

DAWN RAIN

One bird song. Where late the others. Doesn't every intensity result in flooding aftermath? The war abscessed, draining the country of all other thought. Advance post-war plan, a photograph developed before it is framed. Image straight to work, no accounting for incoherent consequences. False causalities, denial of indeterminacy. They are enemies, we'll get them fast, we'll get out faster. *All will be well with prayer*. The rapture, the Roman zeal of *a mors*. The one bird stops singing. The bowers of the greening tree vibrate. The sky dips lower. Most people on earth worry about mortality, not immortality, or how history pans out. You look fully alive, you look vibrant, you look like a war isn't about to break the world into pieces pieces pieces. This word processor, incapable of accepting more than one piece, inserts squiggly red lines under repetitions, capitalizes the uncapitaled. Capital invaded even the keystroke. Who intervenes on the interventionists? A government goes after an enemy it installed itself. A prime minister is assassinated this time, no archduke. A government imagines other countries, its own intelligence knows better. A tribe is not a country, though sovereign and inviolable. A sudden flock of birds takes cover. The treetops, a choir loft, a pulsing body of sopranos. A fog. Assassin behind the wheel, driving at top speed toward the trunk, next to the *femme fatale*, victim of her own wiles. Sailing over the cliff. Captured forever in celluloid, a form of immortality.

FOREST OF DAWNS

I was living in a forest of dawns. The recent past shining brighter than the present. Body in one, mind in another. What a stretch of the imagination! I was living in a you that no longer existed for an I. As though the four would merge in the future, defying pronouns and their hopeless referents. Yet hope permeated the present. This was acknowledged as a false hope, but anticipatory earnings thrive on so little. The past had been looted. Temples, statues, icons, liquor, Arabian horses, precious stones, clay pots that carried water from real mirages. Yet as one who lives with phantoms, an I lived. The infrequent communiqués received from beneath the surface were enough. Language formed a carapace, often protecting itself from the present. I would walk into a room unseen, invisibly dressed. I could not understand why other persons could not see a me, but only a disembodied complicitor. To my "self" I appeared completely laminated, confidently one. A phone call would confirm the existence of the words I, you, us, them. The dial tone then annihilated all phonemes and their suffixes. The days filled themselves with choleric tunes, sounds from planets so far away from earth's orbit, pre-harmonic, yet not inaudible. The skin creased, deepening its own knowledge of the past. How could I have mistaken the unequal for the equal? A terrible mathematical indiscretion, a mistake, an answer without a demonstrated process which no teacher in her right mind would accept. At times all solutions seemed further falsehood, as though one had peeked onto another's paper for the answer which was wrong to begin with. Yet the felt lived in its own body, a dense forest of desired trees recently planted and currently still in bloom. Could I have mistaken tree for bloom? As though it had only a season, then died. Everyone knew this, yet kept living as long as possible. Everyone but the first and second person pronouns seemed sure. The ground solid, the branches perpetually restless. A horizon rising through the reign.

THE YOUNG KEEP DYING ABROAD AND AT HOME

Tired anemone shoots last bloom
Neither lassitude nor industry
Impress the machinery
Of neat hedges & Kalashnikovs
Hand over those scissors to cut the hair
Of graves one strand at a time
Something blazing some city razed no this
Fatigue has a name abhor dolor honor
Push brooms galore sap-soaked leaves
The inevitable debris of time gum
Wrappers quarters to account for
Inflation petrified fish bone so
Far from the sea a 9 mm shell
And thee fair garden so far from hell

SELF PORTRAIT

First Carl says to butter 'em up with margarine produced off shore, then slither into multiple layers of the accusative, invoking the felonies of Satan and how we dropped peanut butter *and jelly* on the devastatees.   Now I'm all dressed up with somewhere to go! (Skirts are in again, Laura).   I'll yodel to Poe, finally accept a pit and a pendulum plus freedom, which, as the song goes, is just another word. I'm God's gift, Mama told me so. [Applause punctuates providential statements, the loving diety behind all life and history.] *(Karl, speak English pulease.)*

I'll say a *name that cannot be spoken.* The jewey Jews won't mind, they love me so.

I was your middlin' student who you tell me metonymizes the country. (This word is so long. How about your average Joe?) Hard tests, inspections, elections, not me, *cheaters never prosper.* I'm never untrue to myself and you. I've got evidence only my senses can detect. There's a bogeyman out there who's bigger than sin. When I drank, I thought he was named Daddy or M. Begin. There's this war, but not a voodoo day goes by that I'm not doing something big and exact. We're taking care of it. We've arrested a true thugation of swarthy ickies. We've terminated the free lunchers. DisneyWorld is a safer place. We're not gonna bother you, my fellow (and fella?) Americans. There are so many other things on your minds, so much else to buy beside speeches.

A new true awaits a boy shot down trying to catch songbirds. And a man in a hole can't hold up his hands very well. Even the horrid suffer *(Karl, these many words are as wide as Texas and my lips are thin)*, in the frail breezes of a thought about a one-way ticket to Mars. So I failed olden history. But history could have failed me. It's over, I'll announce. Caput. Goodie, we don't have to memorize dates anymore. We don't like the rules, so we change 'em.   Or, before we send them good-for-nothing-else *pobrecitos* to the next libertacious war, repeat: A fetus conceived a few weeks ago has the right to a jury trial.

SOLUTION SIMULACRA

Deepening shades fall into *crepuscula*, says the beautiful Sandinista exiled in a country that twilighted her revolution.

Fresh war beckoned with its siren calls, one wanted to think in one's own words, even nurse the melancholy dusk with tender coos of don't *cry baby don't cry*. Another mother for breast suck a baby duck in the tub.

So many award winners present, each kissing a cheek and one bought the drinks so they could argue toward solution.

New translation of the *I Ching* with plastic coins and "wise person."

The law of remedies sits in her tree. The revolutionary shows no surprise.

Ghosts of the Ottoman Empire survey the imminent damage—jealous, zealous, and poised to advise. Frustrated with one's adversary? Annihilate him. Otherwise, one will remain impotent, and that will disturb one's sleep. Empire is an issue of temperament. Then the work begins.

First, suck all the money out of the house to fashion the *haute couture* weapons. Buy pushpins. Color in the sections of the world one would like to have. Make lines of routes and show how troops move. (Here is where pushpins come in handy.) Demand that first adversary hand over his arms and the arms of all his doubles, and send them Fed Ex. When they arrive, thank him, and demand he do the same with his head and the heads of all his doubles and theirs. When they arrive, have these parts well-photographed in color and printed on the front page of *The New York Times* and every other medium will follow suit. Eliminate the text. No one wants to read seventeen pages about reasons. Reading is treason in a simulated solution. Repeat as necessary.

DECREE

The statute of those particular illuminations ran out
A bank runs out of money a runner out of breath
a vehicle out of gas a people out of food
capitalism out of order. Try prophecy

It worked previous centuries but now
Nobody from then knows the trouble we've seen
Nailed jailed scaled sold doled out
An octave of lies wider than the sky

With a mind outside a body the mime insists
Repeat Repeat Repeat Liberty
A voice at last freed, genetically modified notions
mating the burdens of feeding breeding rogue nations

Say your gilded matins at night
Get your density out of my trigger happy beauty
And don't hurt the believers.   Just stop shame
Worse than faithless are the miserated

Trees thrive inside stanchions unmoved by
the coalition of the milling and filling
Discontinued visceral hypersensitivity
caused by hurricane blowing one's top off

The weather calms to memory
Certain objects depose from their prominent pedestals
Pre-emptive present now hyphenated
from the vast past bound to leave traceless grace

CLUSTER THEORIES

fresh water ≈≈≈≈≈≈≈≈≈≈≈a chunk off the icy dicey

Émigré Martians
                        Now American
                                        Politicians
Everything's a clue

        but where's the mystery?

History   antique medium   no more owned

        by the winner   that sinner   and his

Stupidly regular dinners

Try to find
                Your true
                                Home

                                        What if time
Flowed backward
~~Unreading each word~~

Color lends weight to
                        Weightlessness
                                        Now red's the new

Dark matter
                A repulsive force
                                        On large scales

And those huge clusters
                                        Refusing
                To behave

When my country looks
                                        Forward it goes *drawkcab*
Check out the photo
                        With Rover's rear
                                                End
                Landed part of the content

Let us count the continents
                        And the incontinents
                                Soon to roam The Last Frontier

And loaf meatly on its astro-turf

    Like take-out?
                        Ready for zip codes and zoning?

Stuff ads moaning girls say you need?
                                Last call at the Hotsy Totsy Club

Pass me a glass of water
                Call if you want to go up

If we don't answer, we're either on another line

                Or helping somebody out the window

Did you say laughs have syllables?

        Why be alone when you can be impulsive

 Macy's now sells
                        Tediomatics

Slices dices chops tedium into smithereens
                                Homeboys and girls

New pearls
         Wanna wear your country's
                  Real neck on your sleeve

So easy to flag you
            Down on my planet

NOT YOU

Once the earth was a lonesome ball with no inhabitants. Then came well-defined heads. Active feeding and predatory behavior followed immediately. A hydra appeared, a net of nerve cells at the mouth of an organism, surrounded by a ring of tentacles that numbed and poisoned its prey. Such a successful addition to life ensured insurance. (One mouth could only soften the kill with its sweet deep.) He said he was an evolved human, but rushed through every part of the act. Are there really closely matched protein sequences? If one cuts off the head of a hydra, the organism regenerates. In other words, gets a new head, new mate. Heads evolved from mouths—the I and the You are primitive, for their mouths are what drew them together. High density of neurons. The front of the animal most efficiently meets its prey. Some are always actively feeding others. Heads became a driving force in evolution. Arms race may emanate from another part of the body. Eat or swim away or hide. If the organism recedes, the aggressor needs to evolve to a greater level, get better at sensing and chasing. Unless it is starving, often what an animal catches, it throws back. Discovers through highly developed senses, not such a good enchant. Something much more evolved awaits from the future, should the future have an opportunity to discover its most loyal devotees and advocates.

SPRING AND ALL

At first one likened the blossoms to snow, and now they open like popcorn in the late morning sun. The impact of such a bomb would destroy eight million people in Bombay in one moment. The reliability of these queens to tell us of spring, here where winter's an intermittent thing. With no smoke, can there be fire? The region is capricious and attracts those who tolerate such behavior on the part of nature. Orphans of summer, cries of spring victory, the large shipment of six foot bags already in preparation. One takes cuttings, brings branches into the house, arranges them in a glass vase so buds will blossom under water. Empires strike and empires strike back. These would soften the heart of a killer, reverse murderous thought, as they sadden the heart of a lover, for obvious reasons. Such drastic action always signals failure. The anise butterfly, wet upon emerging, hesitates to leave the human finger, where it perches startled at its own existence. The closer to death, the closer the emperors cite from their holy scriptures. But the moment one shakes the tree, the blossoms fall.

CARGO CONTENTS

What's in them? Every container is just the beginning of beauty. Every blue, yellow, green, red, black, grey, pink potentially contains Them and what They might do.

The ports are vulnerable, the cold sherry refreshing, the weightless freight unbearable. Imagining affectionate riches right over the horizon or stowed away in a lavender boat with a runcible spoon. So myopic, the horizon is in front of one's nose. The Greek actor wore many masks, as he might have to play numerous roles. The child turned and murmured *the voice, without instruments, is the purest music.* There would be no way to make steel opaque or x-ray every shipment. To a child, a dog is for walking love, not sniffing around containers. Soon much of what she imagines will be shipwrecked and what floats to shore enough to build a symphony. Adults in charge of eliminating children in charge of everything hidden in the containers. What if you don't like the sound of a person's voice? What if a person's voice says, this is it, you're the recitative I'm dying for and with. Language is based on the conditional. Music is the only invisible refuge. Various memos were ignored or minimized, various varied clues from sources too unreliable to verify. Shoes, tapes, papers, socks, movies, books, cards, bills. These couldn't bring down a country. They could only illustrate the contents of the cargo. What's next? Every smiling Mesopotamian reminds the coast guard that terror is just the beginning of beauty. Why smile as you are escorted away. We don't speak in paragraphs. Each single mercenary is terrible. Operatives, the knowing brutes aware that we don't feel securely at home, need a single gesture to carry out commands within our interpreted world. Ought not these oldest sufferings of ours be yielding more music by now?

MESSAGE TO LEGATEE

I does not want to go to war. And you don't either. What does I want? I does not want to make odes. Wilfred Owen downed in elegy. Several deer appear among the tall grasses, look up and keep chewing. I wants to get down to brass tacks and trombones and leave the spit shine behind. What does we want? We doesn't exist. To govern is make decisions that have little to do with I's and We's. The man who boos at operas, a fanatic? I moves like a scorpion saving I's best venom for the worst crises. Emperors could learn from the animal world.   Soon I will be under house and garden, time runs and dies of an attack at any moment, so it's good that there is at least one Zionist who took Ecstasy. One and one do not make we, we is not a mathematical equation, but an idea whose time has never come. Here is a list of important maladies that may affect anyone, including decent, law-abiding citizens:

Pa-feng: phobic fear of wind and cold in Chinese patients
Hwa-byung: suppressed-anger syndrome in Korean patients
Latah: psychosis leading to uncontrollable mimicking of others suffered by Malaysian and Indonesian patients
Erectile dysfunction: suppressed anger suffered in all patients, plus bad circulation on account of drugs for the mind that suppress anger
Familial dysfunction: see above
Dissident ayatollahs: talk back big sheik small tribe
Fatwah: you jihad infidel! you should know this by now

Why does night fall? Why not envelop? Where does it fall from? I understands why sun rises, which is also false, but darkness permeates. You are always asking too many questions, and I is incapable of answering them in the rapidity of this century.

Dear Legatee, This is How it Be:

Your buds have bloomed so soon. The sky behind them is foreground; in the background, all possible futures. If they allow it. The pronouns, their referents, and their tenses about to act now. You and I aren't them. They are not Representative of I nor You, compelled to abide and defy. Now yodel that thirty-word synopsis of Late Capitalism and Its Ills, will you?

TREE

Everyone continues to bark up the wrong tree. But there's a whole forest out there, you say. He could stop at every sapling, Whas' happening, baby? to deaf limbs. It has come to my attention that trees do not move unless under severe distress. Only leaves and branches bend with the times, indifferently. So why choose trees in the first place. Envy of roots, knowing the tall are free. Remedy lived in one. Old growth≠old money landed and in charge. Nouveau nix. One likes to follow the thoughts of an agile branch of thought even if one cannot. Happy Wednesday, thank you, hello! Weren't you at the Psychic Fair last week with a frizzy-haired child? Sorry, my heart weighs a ton, and they're checking baggage so carefully these days.   Or, I AM RADIO ACTIVE, DON'T TOUCH ME. One never wonders, only invents an image of what a beloved might do at this very moment. A private movie theater with twelve screens.   About those trees. Cut down one redwood around here, and you're an instant leper. But it was too close to the house, he cries. Too bad, move the house. And quit that barking. Find another tree to pick on. A mean lady planted live oaks to deaden her neighbor's view. If two people who live three feet from one another can't come to terms, then? Me Me Me a whole table of them. I gave up sugar, I was an addict. You see, I'm not even taking any rice. But chicken and rice are nice, she says. Oh no, one bite and I go to hell. She understands, nods, waiting to be asked, And what did you give up, do, think, want? The right tree, *wuff wuff.* The very right tree.

SMOKING BANNED TWENTY FEET FROM DOORWAY

Heart red purple good arteries, no smoke
Promised pay no need to announce gay

While I wait to ship off to war
I can personally be misperceived of details

Attend a venue called
Low Fat Mood Food

At a local hang no cover girls
Provide soulful rib grooves

A sepia ad promising
Steps to Improve Your Social Life

Dive into our Happy Waters
Subvert the Dominatrix

Play Accordion, Shop in the Name of Love
This sounds good to an absolute beginner

Pressing on keys and squeezing the honey
Ban normality. A continuum ending in nuts

How come it took me so long
To get it? Oh look, other orders

Embrace Change, Love Your Mother
Be Dumb than Def. I could attend Spank

One night at a neighborhood bar
Savant Guard the next

If I like sawdust, the following features
Pedestrian. Are these booking agents

College dudes enjoying crudités a la mode?
Oh how I wish

I could get away
With the sweet tea once more

Hide under the bed kiss kiss or
Draw in wet cement

Thank you, oh Lord, for reminding me
Of my Immortality

What do these (Hot and Horny) Girls
From the papers actually do?

Chat, yes a battalion of words
That blurs war zones

Now for the Horoscope
"Can do, will do, must do

"This week Jupiter provides a humorous bent
So expect he-haw in the tent"

Apartment for sale
Not yet built

A dream of home own
Tone up for the holidays

 I got scabies, sorry baby it
Spreads when scratched

Revealing more of the dread
Disintegration of public smooching

Basic training slipping
Off its own ground

Here's one for
www.loveme.com

Where you can meet
Beautiful Foreign Women

Russian, Latvian as seen on
MTV, Time

And all you wrongfully terminated
Retaliate! Contact your nearest recruiter

Pull yourself through a ponder
Make your family's heart grow fonder

IN AND OUT

This guy's going to drown in those pools he's wanting. And if he dives into that oily fountain of youth again, oh boy, shallows crack head. Isn't it enough that plums plop and he barely feels them? All the noses of all the courtiers seem to be growing. Why o why has the Emperor gone to Nigeria in those old clothes. 6.0 hours in Botswana. *Congratulations, Uganda, 3.25 hours, we think you're doing a marvelous job of containing the deadly disease.* .25 hour a la **Maison Des Esclaves** , Senegal, *very emotional, very touching.*

One stumbles along the same highway as one's predecessors. And suddenly makes new mistakes wearing different shoes. Pull out too soon, stick around too long, and a few snipers turn into a whole resistance. A bicycle rider can't help it if his vehicle flattens a slow lizard. Your locked datum are getting in my way, time to cut them.

Amp up the frenzy to which each scene builds? Get in get out and leave 'em wanting. This could be the last of many or the first of several more, who can tell when the stakes aren't on the table, even planted as they should be, on solid ground. The slick reign of terror could be cracking, the big fibs spreading their roots and lifting the cement. Did you or did you not have relations with those rogues? I did not, he will insist emphatically. How come you can't find them? Where'd they go? To a luxury island called Undisclosed Location?

New *DSM* entry-- petrocentricity: pathological compulsion to send the young and fresh to do one's killing for an unctuous, viscose combustible substance.

Not to mention rob nests of the victims' treasures. But that's just excuse beneath subtext beneath the simple word called Mine. You mean you don't speak English?

A good sentence is a good sandwich, hold the adjectives. Easy on the adverbs. Heavy on the verbs. Let's ask the rewind girl to show us the film of the staged event on the theater of operations. Ah yes, look at that. A reel of lies as big as the screen.

NO

Sumptuary sounds sumptuous not financial. What if one were covalent rather than ambivalent, two atoms in a chemical compound sharing electrons. Both hands of the same body rather than two minds of the same body stuck together, inseparable. Should have been separated at birth. Should have been taught the distinct meanings of Yes and No. If so, would have acted on one and not both. Would have acted sumptuarily while sumptuously offering those diamonds and sapphires. Among the ambivalent, money is not the issue. So used to cheap wine doesn't know good, says good to everything. Nice to everything else. Around such a person, one enjoys being bad bad bad. In order not to be nice. In order to alter the No inherent in Maybe. Some people were never meant to be friends. Friendship outlasts even one's children, who were never meant to be friends. In some countries, they die quite early and long before their parents. Even in this country. The parent of a dead child wishes to jump into the grave with the child. Why not? Something unnatural has occurred, or is it guilt for the living on? What is natural? Does the parent of a dead child feel mortality the way a friend feels, the way a child feels when a parent dies first? One is next in line. Step up to the plate. What is your batting average? Will we keep you or trade you next season? Will you retire young and rich or young and done? If you are done, you give into the gurney that carries you across the River Styx. It's there for you, moving along on wheels. There are no more rivers to the underworld. Pain and forty-five minutes later, you're there. What was to live for, your dying body asks your soul? Giving in is a form of suicide. Not giving in is the Puritan ethic one is supposed to abide. However, much of the world knows nothing about Puritan. Much of the world imagines death as beauty. Killed into beauty. As though it were an art.

RENAME

this language problem

      apprehend the moan

            in a syllable of sound

launching new strikes

      turns upon itself

the direct object in Spanish

      caresses the subject   in English

the subject protects the direct object

though any I   would like   protection

      the gift that was   rescinds

hope is now intransitive

      the words inside you   mirror

         the worlds outside   or   vice verso

sudden objects

      shadow buds

about to bloom   in the conditional morning

      night arrests the day

    the branch snaps

felled by fear

    of the progressive   leaves

what is   the verb between them

    a game too soon to call

called back

    by a terrible preterite

some night falls into morning

    they will say

he threw it all away

    the banquet before

the unconjugated future

goal   and the goalie's last chance

    doubt   a false fuel   a dramatic tool

I is among them

    I shuns them

I had wished for a different

      personality borne   of a warless time

everything actually turns right   taking its time

      a mandatory toll   to cross the bridge

of reversals   often rehearsed

                  lived through

dead

      assassins of tenderness   preventing an us from

 love   a famous verb

      a we struggles to live

            transitively

with the desire for   ever   always

      gripping the margins

of a foreign bed

THE REAL THING

An innate preference for the represented subject over the real thing
Henry James

Voluptuous thought. Wrapping around the mind like legs. Bending to one's every image, more flexible and seductive than argument. So what that Plato waries all forms of rapture other than reason. And that other derangement called Eros. This thought is not sexual but luxurious play. A single idea. Freed from causality. I wants the substance of it, want it named. Cannot recover it from dream. Nor describe. Often senses evade language. I'm serious, you might be on a spree. But this page is writing to survive. To endure the inability to express the most important moments. Is there no mercy in you? Will you say, like a peasant pedant, good enough but not Tolstoy? Over time, this had nothing to do with the erosion of their lives. His resistance to black silk teddies disunited them. But comparisons such as these do not begin to be or not to be. One's endeavor makes a delayed return to earth.   My dearest, you say the writing often craves beauty. Why not? It's hardly the exclusive domain of the opposite sex. Her legs roundly muscular, cream thighs, fingers made for striking keys, face imperfectly lucent, as if pores were doors to miniature insights. Only the slightest disproportion. Such a mind. Depth after depth, unfathomable. Those lips too, cracked by speech. A real image. Immortal and nothing like the person herself, that temporal half-mute mirage, that worker, that daughter, that mother, that lover—a being whose desire could save or destroy the vicinity.

SAPPHO SAYS

for E.B.

People gossip about time

You know this place:
A teetering brink

Mind hears chanting
Bare wave

A new slip
of victory

And your petticoats adrift!
                              Blue plans seep thru
          Complicated unravel
                Favored daughter

                                        True find

Pride works hard
Fits into any tight spot

Did I say how the world
is a word problem with
theorem and proof?

I take it back
While you're away

That tyrant will fall down
His bare bottom scraping along
Harsh stones

SAPPHO RECONSIDERS

Born again into fallacy
Raised by the best minds
And streets

Teetering brink
Water's been everywhere

Dissolved ancient ruinated

A new cloak

No victory

Sea plans see thru

Those wars

Even before Agamemnon, Odysseus, Helen
Who is true

Enter other metrics
Molesting tongue

Geometry
in which all shapes
lose their form

Inert enchant

Fierce drop
Liar puppet olive thief

That man will fall down
His bare bottom scraping along
Spiked stones

BIRD, WAR, CHAINSAW

can't count

        count on

    numbers

          leaves

      birds say : they're taking us down

            Holy Fallujah!

how many say the branches

              to the occupiers &

    stop making our beds

        they're our beds

      count the severed

                nests from torsos

you can't

      make alive

        again

TIRED OF LIVING YOUR LIFE?

Let us live it for you! Trust the experts, Life Livers, a group of highly trained, skilled professionals lifers. We will wake up for you in the morning, kiss your mate or pet goodbye, take your children to school, commute to your work, work at your job, pick up take out or cook (depending upon your preferences), bring in your car for service, pick up your clothes at the cleaners, attend your children's sports events, as well as school plays, open houses, talks with teachers. No need to wait in the outer chamber of the Humane Society, where your child has volunteered and must be accompanied by an adult, only to be forced to listen to yowls and yappings of snarling canines. We'll cover for you. Why attend four hour violin, piano, cello recitals? Why bake cookies, especially in this low-carb era? Why drive five hours to Camp Boolaboo, only to return in two weeks to sit through a three-hour production of children in clown suits falling off stilts? Tired of packing lunches, signing up for summer camps in January, enforcing homework? We are especially noted for our ability to deal with The Dark Years, when teenagers often hate their parents and consider becoming emancipated minors. Why have them hate you when you can let them hate us? Why shop? Why drive to the beach during traffic on a Sunday morning? Why visit a railroad museum when all you'd like to do is curl up and sleep? Why go through the agony of helping a high school senior fill out applications for college? We can do this work in a matter of hours, retaining calm and placid relations with your hormonally imbalanced offspring. Why teach your sixteen year old to drive only to have him/her/it burst into tears at your mild critiques of his/her/its parallel parking and failure to signal? We have been through this for decades and we never flinch. Why go through the misery of a long or short-term affair when we can do it for you? Our crew includes highly seductive individuals who will suffer the heartbreak, humiliation, or disgust of the break up. And our staff is trained in occupations ranging from Astrophysicist to Zoo Keeper, from Single Mom to Extended Family, from coast to coast, from local to multinational. We have been through this for decades and we never flinch. We have been through layoffs, divorces, lack of promotions, promotions, evictions, work-aholism, brises, bar mitzvahs, confirmations, *quinceañeras*, weddings, IRS audits (what stress!), smarmy real estate agents, home purchases, mortgages, bills, bathroom remodels, drug addiction, rehab programs, diets, spousal abuse, lawsuits, prison sentences, exercise programs, years of therapy, earthquakes, roof rats, new foundations, termites, felled trees, monsoons, corrupt politicians, cutbacks, drawbacks, blowbacks, the sexed up and sexless years. We know how to maintain long-term friendships, contacts, connections. We have experts who struggle for you, to find loans and scholarships for the college years, pay off debts, assemble cheap shit Danish furniture for your children's first apartments. Mid-life crises? Let us take the burden off you, as our highly skilled staff has researched remedies as ancient as Cleopatra. Repulsed by skiing, snowboarding, snorkeling, cross country biking, eco-tourism, the churches of Europe, the mosques of Arabia, the shrines of Asia? Disgusted by drug wars, drive-bys, poverty, starvation, orphans living in the streets? We have a fleet of suffering workers at the ready. We are especially experienced in the early, tragic death of family members, good friends, the later years of parents turning into infants, and the inevitable last days filled with pipes and tubes and monitors and images of the body's functions. We don't just let your parents die—we stroke their hands as their opiated eyes barely recognize us. Why should they recognize us? If you can afford us, we work for you, while you don't have to bother! For additional fees, we can even die for you. You can attend your own funeral, holding a black umbrella in the rain, watching loved ones weep. And then you can be free to live the life you always dreamed of. Our operators are on duty 24/7. The first 3 minutes are toll free. An experienced agent will visit you at home and together you will create your future. Why wait! Call now!

VAL U

Lovely day, luv. Line up the flower stands. Side the mandatory roads with pre-pacs, big Red Bows. E-mail Her, an "easy way" to say 'I want your hot bod now'. The nurse takes a broom to a 65-year-old guy under 78-year-old Granny's bed. Please send apricot roses, not those grown under toxic conditions for the pickers. Cause my luv is not like a red rose. On this day, one may explain "Object Relations Theory" to 18-year-olds, the pre-narrative screen of lovies, cut off from the natal breast. Shadow was his name and he lived a loved life. Until one evening, he was left behind, as though modernity had freed him. It's all about Me, and I is paying you, so why are you inserting yourself into my resumé? The day turns out somewhat obscene. That is, reports of the beloved in vain. Yet one keeps loving intransitively in the midst of this unlanguaged event. The guy killer in the film always leaves a spread flower on the body. This doesn't happen off-screen.

Bereft of what one desires, such as a bouquet of the wildest blooms of February. Silence, like nature, with its own plans. How many countries celebrate this day? Those who haven't murdered Venus outright, those whose arrows have not turned nuclear. Red wine, pink cookies, have another, I is talking now and wants to be heard and seen in color.

That paradise we once visited not so heavenly. As a biological party pooper, I must tell you that one drop of water viewed under a microscope mimics a microbial heart.

Still a dear they did love. Possibly artificial selves wrapped around trompe-l'oeil. Yet how much more could they have done, considering the early damages. Promise? Possibly? Impossibly? Possibly? Impossibly?

Each ripped petal flutters to the anonymous pavement.

ADDICTION

One who once waited for the mailman every day, who felt that a day without mail was a sad day, who stood behind gauzy curtains in front of opaque drapes in childish anticipation for the sound of the wooden lid slapping the box, or years later, perched on the steps and teased the postman for wearing shorts and not bringing any good mail, how come no money, how come no letter, no invite, and why all these advertisements for tires, file cabinets, sheets, gold jewelry, white sales, low mortgages, free credit cards, publish your own book, put your money in our bank, chain saw specials, save now subscribe for two years, blow your photo up to poster size for Christmas, half price sale at SportsWorld, genuine pashmina shawls for a pittance, etc. One who one waited for the mail—the palpable, rippable, recyclable, low postage, no postage, postage due—now awaits e-mail. A term the French cannot abide, a signal dispersed in space, a message of acceptance, rejection, divorce, chit chat, far away friends, old acquaintances, photos included, attachments attached, favors asked and favors returned, emotive avoidance due to scant inflection in the modus operandi, get togethers and break ups, endearments and chastisements, pop ups offering Christian financial assistance, Christian mortgage rates, Christian dates, camcord computer student displaying her breasts, pop up blockers, free trip to Las Vegas, prizes, surprises, disguises, vitamins and minerals, sanctifications and manifestations of the news, the blues, who's who in the world of dog grooming. Now, if there is no e-mail, or it isn't the desired e-mail (though most important matters still arrive via telephone calls and the blessed human voice), one feels zero. After all, it's an on-off system. One does not like receiving long attachments which one has to print out at one's expense and time, anymore than one liked receiving long, unanswerable requests for money in the outdoor mailbox. And yet, e-mail arrives at any moment, night or day, producing round the clock nervous anticipation, unlike the post which has certain parameters of anxiety, Sundays off, a changing hour, depending upon the route, the mailman, and forces beyond one's control. But this sort of communiqué, this screen that now even alerts the user of a message on its way, is addiction. Try living without it for one day and watch the results. DT's, moral collapse, wakeful nights, somnolent days. One has to leave to house in order to not want it. One has to take a trip to a country that does not have internet cafes. One has to climb a mountain and listen to birdsong--a cold turkey cure for this terrible and time devouring malady.

DON'T KEEP

white heat from dark
mind wants rhyme
go together salt & pepper

hair   staircase   seems
you sew what you: re:
a white fire

gray ashes
and two beds   who's been
sleeping

in the same room you
half 'n half kids
the way the world will be

I guarantees just you see
not con
just fusion

of the body politic
mix up the race toward
the present's future

don't black me out
you're my best church and
I is mad at I's country

some trees
felled for profit
not stop building

but what
about traffic
in traffic in

religion check
the donation box
know it elects

bad grammar
dumb guns

LIBERATION AFTER LIBERATION

No jungles junk jingles singles bars just Mars around here. Marsh people drained to a desert the size of New Jersey. No cuchi tunnels copter fire cop a feel monkeys on anyone's back. Nobody's going to forgive and make nice later, move to California and open restaurants and nail parlors. Infested by everyone and their mothers since before time began, they might have even invented time taxes and death. Imagine the grudge sludge oil yummy desertification soil degradation no *dinar*. Just pull up an Ottoman and relax your tassels. Dog tags won't rust. Unable to dust fingerprints off a sand dune twice the size of Idaho hold the potatoes. You need blowjob you get blowback. No backing out now if you want dessert. What's in a name, a bomb by any other blowing up a face in the marketplace would stink the same. Genghis Khan so open to stories. Then the unnarrated Tartars arrived with their saucy blood busy for forty days, smashing up canals and pots. *Political confusion, rapid deterioration of settled agriculture leading to growth of tribally based pastoral nomadism.* History always sounds familiar. But don't blame the rapee for the rape, if you please. This is just one mini-series in a long civilization. Credit is due to the genes that managed memory. Wouldn't you know it, a flood then a plague did them in again, then those reclining Ottos pointed from a comfy spot in the parlour. And the Young Turks, in cahoots with zee Germans.

Kingdoms kingdoms kingdoms, horses repeat to themselves when it looks like they're chewing. Short wars on hungry people the sheiks eat good.

It's 5:45 a.m., March 23, 2003. Do you know where your child is? Firing a Tomahawk, ma'am. First casualty: Native American Private Private.

And now poor coda, you're as long as a whole symphony. Perhaps till infinity.

No gorillas no mist. Sad recruits dodge the exploding stage. The fourth wall of this theater is pretty pissed at non-union wages. The rations are so, well, icky. The women so unfuckable. Morale not high or low, just not. WMD? PTSD? PMS?. You guys were told to take a city, so turn off that girlie tearduct and go peacekeep. Go pile up bricks, go bang your pricks against the wall if you're bored. What did anyone want here for 4000 years? War after war, you really can't get out to visit. No place to hide. Can't understand snide remarks. If the people curse, they spit. If they smile, it doesn't show.

MEDICATE SPECIFIC

I am a soldier in the war and I am a person. Who left persons behind. I drink to medicate the specific. I find a vein and mine it to medicate the specific. All goes well except the specific. I have been commanded, I am afraid, I will kill, this is against my nature, so I must obey the order and remain lonely in my specific anti-desire. I do not wish to maim others; however, I was promised certain things, such as. When the band plays I forget. I go along, I hold myself erect, I enter the body of another country and I am ready. But I am scared. *This hour I tell things in confidence/ I might not tell everybody, but I will tell you.* Like water, I have been everywhere I am needed. I wish to be needed. I wish to be a part of the human race, though I am asked to do things that seem in- and un-human. *We are all animals, though we behave worse than them.* I have to ignore this aspect of the current conflict. I am therefore I am. I was told, I was promised, I showed up. In order to do what I do, I medicate myself. How else could I do it. How else could I live among those who do what I do not really wish to do or be. You don't know me, you would never know me, I am unknowable, unseen, your servant, your loyalty, your surrogate. I carry the mutation of war in me. I deliver. War is born dead. I nurse it. I kill for it, defending what I deliver. Please understand. I am an ordinary. I am a person. I is I is I is and will be. Sweet Mary, who bore Jesus, who bore our savior. Help me now. Dear You at Home: Your photographs, in my pocket, do not marry anyone else, while I'm gone. Do not forsake me. I carry you with me. The thought of you enables me to go on. This has been written a million times and a million times women have written or not written back. No deceit just fatigue. I wear those too, camouflage. The forest, I am to resemble it, I am to deforest it, I am to be it, I am to be you in your stead. However, I know you do not want my service, you would rather I not be here, and I too would rather not. I signed up, I said Yes, it did not subtract from my love of you. Sweet You, whoever. Please forgive me, I will kill and I will kill again and it will be legal, it will be the "enemy," it will disable, destroy, shock, decivilize, I did not choose the specific consequences, but I do medicate the specific, with wine with pill with needle with anything to shut out the wound of the wounding. No history will forgive me, no history will absolve me, no history cares for me, do you care for me, do you love me. Say yes, say yes, say yes.

SEPTEMBER LAYED BARE, AN AUTUMN BRIDE

hurricanes K & R

After the wave theater, the crowd excites
                A chill reception sets off white heat

Gloved queens and kings
                And clipped dikes without red playlocks

Your tentative roles still shaking with what?
                Devotees, evacuees, displaced, misplaced

Where's your baby? I'd like to know too
                Whose doll floats down the accidental river

The brand new Diaspora
                Dry arroyo bayou

You swim? You sink or
                Wait in line for tickets

Flame says to ice melting
                Any day on each breach the other

Excuse me for my compensatory fire
                A branch with no bird you recognize

All gone. Liars still hide in the ivy
                Blues flees with the flown to moan in Utah

I should be used to you by now
                You've always leaned back germanically

Born into the wrong branch of humans
                        Gaining by ignore, shrink in a wake

A safer heat shrouds the
                Dreamed continents

Unable to match blood wedding
                        Flotillas from a corrupt bay

BEGIN

Perhaps dawn has dawned. And there is no in between now until another day or twilight. Nature plays out, strictly, salaciously, imperatively if one watches shoots and branches. After a few days of not waking at dawn, not faking as language loves to, one is ready for other enchantments. The military recruits early, and I stayed private for much too late. Recently, I have been promoted to an undeclared rank. I could have been demoted, only today the temperature is heating up and all the hard blocks are melting fluids. Power often impoverishes itself unwittingly. The rest of the world may put a quick stop on the party's greedy tentacles. Poor, a word, like love, should be banned for its inherent passivity and injustice. Words should always live beyond their means, take strong action, walk right off the page and drag the princess home by the hair, if necessary.

Thirty-second pitch for a new movie: Man and woman separate. *They meet again after the war*. One could build that one up into a real triangle. Woman demands love is a verb. Man only knows immediate present tense, dreams scenes, yells out in his sleep, *Nobody's seen the dog bites I've witnessed*. And his heart is none too sound, considering the ache.

You can guess the ending? Well, it's not going to go like that. The producers have promised to not reveal a thing, and the coming attractions limit themselves to a minute of heightened suspense, instead of the entire movie cut up into cubist collage.

One can never summarize the most important things. Like the sky, what to say about it. Like why one war or love abandons the struggle and another begins.

Revamped, retooled, and remembered fondly, painfully, or with a terror that forces the one and the many to watch the mesmerizing theatre of operations quite carefully for long time.

Gloria Frym was born in Brooklyn and lives in Berkeley. Her last book of poems, *Homeless At Home*, won an American Book Award. She is the author of two critically acclaimed collections of short stories, *Distance No Object* and *How I Learned*, as well as several volumes of poetry, and essays, reviews and articles on literature, photography and other visual media. She teaches at California College of the Arts in the Bay Area.

UNITED ARTISTS BOOKS

Across the Big Map by Ruth Altmann $12.00
Judyism by Jim Brodey $8.00
Join the Planets by Reed Bye $14.00
The California Papers by Steve Carey $8.00
Personal Effects by Charlotte Carter $8.00
The Fox by Jack Collom $10.00
Columbus Square Journal by William Corbett $10.00
Solution Simulacra by Gloria Frym $14.00
Smoking in the Twilight Bar by Barbara Henning $8.00
Love Makes Thinking Dark by Barbara Henning $10.00
Liquid Affairs by Mitch Highfill $10.00
Poems for the Whole Family by Daniel Krakauer $8.00
Head by Bill Kushner $8.00
Love Uncut by Bill Kushner $8.00
That April by Bill Kushner $12.00
One at a Time by Gary Lenhart $10.00
Another Smashed Pinecone by Bernadette Mayer $10.00
Red Book in Three Parts by Bernadette Mayer $8.00
Something to Hold On To by Dennis Moritz $8.00
Songs for the Unborn Second Baby by Alice Notley $12.00
Fool Consciousness by Liam O'Gallagher $8.00
Cleaning Up New York by Bob Rosenthal $10.00
Political Conditions/Physical States by Tom Savage $10.00
In the Heart of the Empire by Harris Schiff $8.00
Along the Rails by Elio Schneeman $10.00
Continuity Girl by Chris Tysh $12.00
Echolalia by George Tysh $10.00
Selected Poems by Charlie Vermont $8.00
Blue Mosque by Anne Waldman $10.00
The Maharajah's Son by Lewis Warsh $12.00
Information from the Surface of Venus by Lewis Warsh $10.00
Reported Missing by Lewis Warsh $8.00
Clairvoyant Journal by Hannah Weiner $12.00
The Fast by Hannah Weiner $10.00

United Artists Books
114 W. 16th Street., 5C
New York, N.Y. 10011
lwarsh@mindspring.com

Small Press Distribution
1341 Seventh St.,
Berkeley, CA 94710
www.spdbooks.org